The
ROYAL FAMILY
Today

The ROYAL FAMILY *Today*

JESSICA HODGE

Photographs by
ANWAR HUSSEIN

LONGMEADOW
P R E S S

This 1993 edition published by
Longmeadow Press
201 High Ridge Road
Stamford CT 06904

Produced by
Brompton Books Corporation
15 Sherwood Place
Greenwich CT 06830

ISBN 0-681-45252-8

Printed in Hong Kong

0 9 8 7 6 5 4 3 2 1

All photographs courtesy Anwar Hussein except page 39 (top),
Bettmann Archive.

PAGE 1: *The Silver Jubilee of 1977, celebrating the 25th anniversary of the
coronation of Queen Elizabeth II, provoked a renewed tide of royalist
fervour, as well as the occasional anti-monarchical grumble.*

PAGE 2: *Pomp and pageantry: the Knights of the ancient Order of the
Garter process to the chapel of the Order, St George's Chapel, Windsor.*

PAGE 5: *The massed bands of the Life Guards leave Admiralty Arch
behind them in the Trooping the Colour ceremony, the kind of vast state
occasion that the British excel at – but which costs a small fortune
to stage.*

CONTENTS

INTRODUCTION

The House of Windsor: essential figurehead, glamorous soap opera or absurd anachronism? The unprecedented events of the last couple of years have not only brought individual members of the Royal Family into the sometimes unwelcome limelight as never before, but have also begun to call into question the whole ethos on which Britain's constitutional monarchy has recently been based. With the almost simultaneous announcements of the divorced Princess Royal's remarriage, the separation of the Prince and Princess of Wales, and a major reduction in the public funding which has supported the jetset lifestyle of some junior royals, radical changes are clearly presaged.

There is no doubt that the role, and indeed future, of the British monarchy has become a subject for real and unprecedented debate, everyone's favourite dinner-party topic. This is partly motivated by the crises and public relations disasters of the last eighteen months, partly by more fundamental questions about the role of the monarchy as a seemingly inflexible institution in a time of change. A poll conducted for a tabloid newspaper by a market research agency suggested that over half the population of Britain want to see changes in the status and functioning of the Royal Family. Already the hacks are turning out articles and paperbacks on the crumbling state of the monarchy; American pulp biographer Kitty Kelley is rumoured to be poised to do a hatchet job on the Duke of Edinburgh; and literary heavyweight A N Wilson, author of an acclaimed life of Tolstoy and a more controversial book on Jesus, has been commissioned to write a serious study of *The Fall of the House of Windsor*. Can any institution survive unscathed such varied and critical attentions? Or is this a temporary preoccupation which will look as dull and outmoded as this year's fashions next year?

Certainly there is nothing new in criticism both of the House of Windsor and of the monarchy as such. Republicanism in Britain has flourished and waned in inverse proportion to the popularity of the reigning sovereign, but it has always fallen short of a real call for the abolition of the monarchy; the republican tradition in Britain has no central tenets to compare with the programme of land, church and legal reform that has formed the basis of government in France. Recent attacks on the monarchy have tended instead to focus on particular complaints. In 1957 Malcolm Muggeridge caused a furore by writing a newspaper article entitled 'Does England Really Need a Queen?', which accused the monarchy of being

LEFT: *The Queen and the Duke of Edinburgh in the gilded state coach.*

ABOVE: *The 1992 Trooping the Colour balcony greeting; Charles and Diana ignore each other, Andrew and Fergie are missing.*

snobbish, isolated and obsolete. In February 1991 *The Sunday Times* devoted its leader column to a swingeing attack on the Royal Family for carrying on regardless when the Gulf War was sending tremors of panic round the globe and British servicemen were at risk. More recently complaints have focused on the large amounts of taxpayers' money devoted to organizing hugely expensive state occasions and keeping flighty young royals in comfort and holidays.

Just before Christmas 1992, Labour MP Tony Benn, who himself renounced a hereditary peerage in order to sit in the House of Commons, reintroduced his Commonwealth of Britain Bill (originally introduced in the previous Parliament). By the terms of this, the Queen would be replaced by an elected president as head of state, the House of Lords would be abolished, the voting age would be lowered from 18 to 16, and national parliaments would be established for England, Scotland and Wales. This has no chance of becoming law, given the constitution of the present House of Commons, but a growing number of MPs are showing interest in debating these issues, above all the role of the monarchy. One of the clauses of the original bill, that the Queen should pay income tax, has effectively been conceded.

The curious fact is that much of the expensive pomp and pageantry linked with the monarchy, and which in a time of austerity is causing more adverse comment than ever

before, is a relatively recent development. When Victoria came to the throne, the crown was not particularly rich and court life not particularly ornate. By the end of her reign, however, the style and ceremonies of the crown had expanded to reflect the growth of empire in the second half of the nineteenth century, creating a splendid, opulent and imperial monarchy. When Elizabeth II succeeded to her ancestress's throne in 1953 she made a conscious decision to put on a show for her coronation in the drab and depressing aftermath of world war. As the nineteenth-century constitutional historian Sir Walter Bagehot wrote:

There are arguments for not having a court, and there are arguments for having a splendid court, but there are no arguments for having a mean court. It is better to spend a million in dazzling when you want to dazzle than three-quarters of a million trying to dazzle and yet not dazzling.

Pageantry became the keynote of the New Elizabethan Age. Weeks of organization are devoted to ensuring that the State Opening of Parliament runs smoothly, but Queen Victoria hardly bothered with the ceremony and it was only later revived by Edward VII. The Trooping of the Colour was originally established in the eighteenth century as the sovereign's birthday parade, but again it only became a regular event under Edward VII, and it was George V who created the form of the present ceremony. Britain has the ceremonies of an imperial monarchy without an empire; many of the real difficulties that face the House of Windsor lie in the increasing divergence between the scale of the monarchy and the diminished reality of 1990s Britain.

Another issue is the sheer number of relations who seem to clutter up the royal stage. The emphasis on public duties performed by royal relations is a relatively recent one, dating from Victoria's withdrawal from public life in the aftermath of her husband Albert's death. Her many children deputized for her on public and ceremonial occasions; individual members began to enjoy a much higher public profile than before, and came to be seen as having their own independent roles. It was in the nineteenth century that the Royal Family as such came to be seen both as a working unit and a moral exemplar to the nation, and this development was reinforced by the reigns of George V (1910-36) and Queen Mary and, after the trauma of the Abdication, of George V's younger son George VI (1937-52) and Queen Elizabeth, now the Queen Mother. Both couples seemed to embody the old-fashioned virtues of fidelity, loyalty and national pride. The errant Duke of Windsor described his father's credo as 'belief in God, the invincibility of the Royal Navy, and the essential rightness of whatever was British.'

Since her husband's death, the Queen Mother has carved out her own very personal niche in the affections of her subjects, particularly those who remember the bravery she and King George VI showed during the Blitz, and continues to impress by her clear enjoyment of life as well as her sheer longevity. The same is perhaps not true of all her grandchildren. Princess Anne is now the Princess Royal, a title bestowed by her mother in recognition of the special place she has earned in public esteem as President of the Save the Children Fund, but she has had her bad patches. In the late 1960s and early 1970s, when Prince Charles was being sheltered as much as possible from the publicity machine that had been invited into the bosom of the Royal Family, Anne became the focus of media attention and felt no compunction, as her father's impatient daughter, about showing her irritation with the result. Similarly Prince Andrew, now the Duke of York, was castigated as 'Randy Andy' for his various, not always subtly handled, liaisons before his insistence on serving in the Falklands War earned him the title of war hero. His marriage to Sarah Ferguson, daughter of Prince Charles's polo manager, seemed ideal – until it fell apart. Prince Edward, too, has been treated to media ribaldry for firmly opting out of the macho army life for which he was so clearly unsuited, and for his devotion to the world of the stage.

In addition to this immediate family, the extended royal family has grown vastly in the last thirty years. Princess Margaret has always maintained that she wants her children to regard themselves as normal mortals; 'My children are not royal', she is quoted as saying, 'they just happen to have an aunt who is the Queen.' And to do them justice, Viscount Linley and Lady Sarah Armstrong-Jones, neither of whom receive any income from public funds, seem quite prepared to get on with the business of earning their own livings. Then there are the cousins, all descended from younger brothers and sisters of the Queen's father George VI. The most senior of these is the Earl of Harewood, who was ostracized by the Court when, in 1967, he was divorced by his wife, the concert pianist Marion Stein (who subsequently remarried Liberal politician Jeremy Thorpe), and married the mother of his youngest son. He was not invited to his niece, Princess Anne's wedding, and had to retire early from his various public positions, although he has since re-etablished a major public role as a patron of opera. Next comes Richard Duke of Gloucester, the architect prince, happily married to a Dutchwoman and with three children. The Duke of Kent, also with three children by his English rose of a wife, the former Katharine Worsley, leads a sober and industrious life within the royal enclave, but his younger brother and sister, Princess Alexandra and Prince Michael, have both had public difficulties with the fact of their royal lineage. The media had a field day when Alexandra's rebellious daughter Marina Ogilvy revealed that she was pregnant but was not planning to marry the father of her baby until after the birth. In the end the baby, given the improbable name of Zenouska, was born in wedlock, and the scandal-mongering seemed decidedly hypocritical in a society where between twenty and thirty percent of all children are born outside marriage. Equally riveting have been the exploits of Prince Michael's glamorous wife, Marie-Christine, determined to maintain a jet-setting lifestyle on a less than princely income.

Much has been made of the role of the press in highlighting the difficulties and disasters that have recently beset various royals. The Calcutt Report on the effectiveness of the British press's regulatory watchdog, the Press Council, found it wholly inadequate and called for statutory curbs on the press's right to free expression, specifically citing reporting of the various royal scandals as instances where supposed self-censorship had not worked. The difficulty with this line of approach as far as the Royal Family is concerned is that it was Buckingham Palace which originally invited the world's press to view royalty as the ultimate family; which decided to present the human face of the Windsors as a counterbalance to royal pomp. The television film *Royal Family*, commissioned in 1968 by the Queen's press secretary and approved by Prince Philip, was concerned to show that, under the formal uniforms and flamboyant robes, the Windsors were nice approachable people just like you and me, taking the dogs for a walk and frying sausages for supper.

For a while this approach worked well; the press was pleased with the greater access afforded it by the Royal Family but did not seek to look behind the well-presented image. But as the world grew less deferential, and the more human royals began to display more human problems, some journalists started to ask more penetrating questions. In 1957 the fact that the Queen and the Duke of Edinburgh spent 19 weeks apart was barely remarked on but in the 1970s, as Princess Margaret flew off to Mustique with Roddy Llewellyn and the Prince of Wales was pursued round England with his latest girlfriend, everything the Royal Family did was newsworthy. By the 1980s, when Prince Edward launched the absurd and embarrassing television show *It's a Royal Knockout* at Alton Towers and the Duchess of York was reported to have knighted a dog at a New York party, they had become too interesting for their own good.

Part of the problem is that the Royal Family do not always seem to be well advised. On the whole the royal entourage is drawn from a small, fairly closely-knit wealthy and/or aristocratic circle, which shows little sign of being in touch with life as it is lived either by the man on the Clapham omnibus or by the single mother in the workplace. The Lord Chamberlain, head of the Queen's Household, is the Earl of Airlie, whose younger brother Sir Angus Ogilvy is married to Princess Alexandra; the Mistress of the Robes, the senior female member of the Household, is the Duchess of Grafton; the Queen's Private Secretary, her closest official adviser, is Sir Robert Fellowes, whose father was the land agent at Sandringham and who is married to Princess Diana's sister Sarah; Ladies of the Bedchamber, who attend the Queen on major public occasions, are always peeresses; Women of the Bedchamber, who do the daily waiting and work two weeks on, four weeks off, have traditionally been the daughters of peers; Equerries, their male equivalent, are almost always serving or retired officers of good birth.

Given all this, it is perhaps easier to understand why there is such real hostility to aspects of the monarchy: unacceptably privileged until very recently in its tax exemptions; unacceptably opulent in its way of living; and unacceptably out of touch with the reality of life in Britain today. These fundamental difficulties have been pointed up by the series of mishaps and scandals that have enlivened the last few years.

In perhaps the most personal and self-abasing speech of her long reign, made toward the end of November 1992 at a lunch given by the Corporation of London at the Guildhall, their handsome eighteenth-century headquarters, the Queen herself in effect accepted that the future of the monarchy needed to be the subject of public debate. The speech

BELOW: *The Queen's Guildhall speech, November 1992, when she made her plea for understanding. Prime Minister John Major, the Lord Mayor of London and Prince Philip all smile in sympathy.*

lasted a mere eight minutes, and its pathos was increased by the fact that it was delivered in a voice made hoarse and painful by a cold. The much-quoted reference to an '*annus horribilis*' was a perversion of the phrase '*annus mirabilis*', year of wonders, applied by contemporaries to the year 1666, when the Fire of London destroyed much of the rat-infested and insanitary medieval city and the Dutch were roundly defeated in the first Anglo-Dutch War. The poet John Dryden described these events in a poem bearing the same title. While Latin scholars sniffed at the Queen's dog Latin, many observers warmed to her plea for understanding:

There can be no doubt, of course, that criticism is good for people and institutions that are part of public life. No institution – City, monarchy, whatever – should expect to be free from the scrutiny of those who give it their loyalty and support, not to mention those who don't. But we are all part of the same fabric of our national society and that scrutiny, by one part of another, can be just as effective if it is made with a touch of gentleness, good humour and understanding . . . He who has never failed to reach perfection has a right to be the harshest critic.

It is perhaps useful to set the increasingly strident criticism of the royals, both as an institution and as individuals, in a more general context. As the Queen said, 1992 was a bad year for a lot of us. The wave of confidence that put the Conservatives back into power in April with a surprisingly large majority barely outlasted the summer and finally died on Black Wednesday, September 16, when the pound lost its place in the European Exchange Rate Mechanism and was

effectively devalued; the Bank of England and the City wobbled, the government looked out of control. Other institutions that came under attack in 1992 included the Church of England, whose waning moral influence and belated and reluctant approval of the ordination of women called into question its role as the established church; the British Broadcasting Corporation, based on the principle of public service and funded by television licence fees but struggling against the proliferation of commercial channels; and Parliament itself, increasingly overshadowed by Europe and big business. While there are specific and individual reasons for the challenges that each of these institutions faces, the fact is that many of them are being forced not just to adapt to new conditions, but to answer fundamental questions about the purpose they serve and their very reason for existing. The lack of a written constitution to provide a degree of underlying continuity makes this process of reassessment or reorientation all the more difficult and painful.

It is undoubtedly true that 1992 was also a bad year for British royalty. Some younger members of the royal family had already earned press and public disapproval with their extravagant lifestyles and frequent holidays, all taken at public expense. The Duchess of York in particular, originally welcomed as a breath of fresh air in the stuffy corridors of 'the Firm', as seasoned courtiers describe the royal establishment, was criticized for her refusal to toe the line, her wild and wacky exploits and expensive tastes. By 1989, from being everyone's favourite redhead, she had been renamed Her Royal Idleness by tabloid journalists catering to fickle public taste. When rumours of an unsuitably close friendship with Texan millionaire Steve Wyatt seemed to be confirmed by the discovery of two-year-old photographs showing the couple on holiday together with the Duchess's two young daughters, it was open season on Fergie. Within two months, on March 19 1992, the *Daily Mail* ran a banner headline 'Andrew and Fergie to part', which was confirmed by a terse announcement from the Palace the next day that a formal separation was under discussion.

The relatively sudden – to outside observers anyway – breakdown of the Yorks' marriage at least distracted media attention for a while from their other favourite sport – speculating on the state of the Prince and Princess of Wales's relationship. But attention was refocused at fever pitch on Charles and Diana with the publication of royal watcher Andrew Morton's sensationally revealing book *Diana, Her True Story*. Based on named interviews with Diana's family and close friends and including exclusive photographs from her father's family album, this carefully researched and coolly written work argued that Diana's love for her husband had been turned first to indifference and then to antipathy by his continuing devotion to an old girlfriend, Camilla Shand, long since married to Colonel Andrew Parker-Bowles. It documented in chilling detail the despair to which knowledge of this liaison drove the young and solitary princess and her hysterical outbursts of reproach, which only served to alienate her quiet, reticent husband. It also recounted her constant battle with bulimia nervosa, an eating disorder in which the sufferer alternately binges on food and then purges herself by deliberate vomiting, and which is usually associated with a poor self-image and lack of confidence. The picture given was

of a young, emotionally immature woman, totally unprepared for the rigours of royal life despite her own fairly privileged background, who received little or no support from her husband, his family, or the courtiers of the royal entourage, and who only very slowly found a role for herself in family- and AIDS-related charities.

Just as the furore created by the Morton book was beginning to die down, the Duchess of York was back in the news. After an island-hopping holiday (which included the irresistibly named island of Phuket) with her children and another American, John Bryan (described as a financial adviser who was guiding her negotiations with Andrew and the royals) she managed to upstage the Royal Ascot opening parade by organizing a picnic alongside the parade route. The last straw, however, was provided by a French paparazzi photographer, whose long-distance photographs of the Duchess and Bryan on holiday in the south of France in August blew once and for all any claim that their relationship was purely platonic. Ironically, the *Daily Mail* was able to publish with impunity these indiscreet pictures of a topless Fergie embracing the balding Bryan, having her back oiled and her toes sucked (source of many delicously unrepeatable jokes), but under tougher French invasion of privacy laws the Duchess and Bryan collected a large damages settlement from the French magazine *Paris Match*.

By now the phrase 'royal soap opera' was in regular use, and royal watchers waited with bated breath for the next indiscretion. Diana's turn again, with the publication of parts of a telephone conversation between a woman and man, presumed to be the Princess of Wales and her old friend James Gilbey (a member of the Gilbey's gin family), which was taped in the first few days of 1990 and nicknamed the Squidgy tapes from the couple's preferred form of endearment. The parts of the conversation made public were of a deeply affectionate but rather inarticulate and inconsequential nature; it was implied even at the time, however, that other more explicit sections were withheld.

A supposedly reconciliatory Mediterranean cruise for the Prince and Princess of Wales was followed by the notorious and disastrous Korean tour. Diana had been reluctant to go, but was persuaded by her royal in-laws to put on a show of solidarity. What was intended to be a successful public relations exercise was scuppered by the world's photographers, however, who were only interested in showing how separately the Prince and Princess operated. The classic pictures of the couple looking bored and miserable in each other's company were actually taken at a Remembrance Day service, not an occasion usually noted for its joyousness, but the message conveyed to an avid public was clear – and, it turned out, accurate.

As if all this was not enough, malign Providence itself decided to take a hand in the afflictions besetting the Windsors. On Friday November 20 a fire which started in the private chapel at Windsor Castle, one of the principal royal residences, destroyed some of the oldest parts of the castle, dating back to the twelfth century. The speed with which the fire took hold, from its starting point in a chapel curtain, defied the efforts of more than 200 firefighters, and raised questions about the exemption from fire regulations enjoyed by royal palaces and castles. What really fuelled the flames,

ABOVE: *Protest placards highlight the contrast between royal luxury and the diminished welfare state.*

however, was Heritage Secretary Peter Brooke's instant pledge that the restoration of Windsor would be paid for from public funds. Suddenly it was too much. Britain was in even deeper recession than in 1991; the pound was in free fall; unemployment was running at almost three million; the plump, contented south-east, with London at its heart, was being hit for the first time by redundancies and foreclosures that paralleled earlier experiences in the rest of the country; and yet there was money to rebuild a stately home for one of the richest families in the world? Many normally loyal and sober citizens shook their heads in disbelief.

One of the more long-running and substantial complaints against the monarchy has been the large sums it draws from state funds and its exemption from taxation. This was not always the case. In 1842 the then Prime Minister, Sir Robert Peel, who introduced peacetime income tax as a temporary measure at the rate of seven pence in the pound to fund his free trade policy, persuaded Queen Victoria that she too should pay tax on her income, from whatever source. This included the Civil List, the annual sum voted by Parliament to the sovereign to cover the immediate expenses of the royal household (as distinct from any private income).

The Civil List was formally established in the reign of William and Mary; in a further development on the accession of George III, the sovereign surrendered his income from crown land, from which the Civil List was drawn, so that any

surplus went to the Exchequer and not to the Crown. Originally the Civil List funded only the sovereign and his immediate family, but as the Royal Family grew in size, so did its requirement for funding. In the ten years 1983-92 Civil List payments more than doubled to £9.79 million ($14.7 million), of which by far the largest sum, £7.9m ($11.8) went to the Queen. The balance represented annual payments to the Duke of Edinburgh; the Queen Mother; Prince Andrew, Prince Edward and the Princess Royal (but not the Prince of Wales, who draws a substantial income from the estates he owns as Duke of Cornwall, on which he already pays 25% to the Treasury voluntarily); Princess Margaret; and Princess Alice.

In 1910 George V managed to exempt the Civil List from taxation, enabling him to build a comfortable private fortune. From Lloyd George's budget of 1906 onward, income tax became an increasingly substantial burden on ordinary citizens as the foundations of the welfare state were laid, but gradually the Royal Family's private income was exempted. By the time George VI succeeded in 1936, the principle of tax exemption for the Crown was established.

As the expansionist eighties gave way to the belt-tightening nineties, however, public attention became increasingly focused on this seeming anomaly, and the promise to restore Windsor at public expense was the last straw. Exactly a week after the fire, Prime Minister John Major answered growing criticism about the cost of the monarchy by announcing that the Queen had already earlier in the year volunteered to pay tax on her annual private income, and that publication of this decision had been delayed while the Treasury, the Inland Revenue and the Palace tried to disentangle her private wealth from her state-owned assets. Unfortunately the result was that, instead of receiving the acclaim that an unprompted decision would have provoked, this looked like succumbing ungraciously to pressure. Another example of bad public relations on the part of both Palace and government. At the same time the Civil List was limited to the Queen, the Duke of Edinburgh and the Queen Mother; although payments will continue to be made to other family members, the Queen will reimburse the state for these from her private income.

This private income is estimated at around a staggering £5m ($7.5m) a year. Private assets include two country residences, Balmoral in Scotland and Sandringham in Norfolk (together valued at about £100m, $150m); the royal racing stables and horses; and a substantial investment folio. State-owned assets, on the other hand, will not be liable for taxation; these include the six royal residences of Windsor Castle, Buckingham Palace, St James's Palace, Kensington Palace, Clarence House and Holyrood House in Edinburgh; the Crown Jewels; gifts from foreign heads of state; and the royal art collection.

However handled, the announcement that the Queen was to pay tax was acclaimed by both supporters and opponents of the monarchy. It seemed that the crown had recognized the need to adapt to changes in circumstances and public mood, and that the period of fierce but often legitimate criticism might be drawing to a close. With her plea for understanding in the Guildhall speech, the Queen seemed to be

BELOW: *The Queen wears some of her magnificent collection of jewellery in Nepal, 1986.*

marking a turning point, the beginning of a period of redefinition and reconstruction. The quiet ending of Princess Anne's marriage to Captain Mark Phillips in April 1992, after more than two and a half years separation, was followed on December 4 by the welcome news that she was to marry the man with whom her name had been linked for several years, particularly following the publication of stolen love letters. He was Commander Timothy Laurence, a naval officer appointed to the royal staff in 1986 to replace Major Hugh Lindsay, tragically killed while on a skiing holiday with the Prince and Princess of Wales. This evidence that some members of the Royal Family were able to conduct their private lives without undue cause for scandal was greeted with relief, though considerable irony was seen in the fact that the divorced daughter of the Head of the Church of England, which does not countenance church marriages for divorcees, should marry again in a Church of Scotland wedding ceremony.

Unfortunately the private lives of several members of the Royal Family again immediately hit the headlines in a way that once more focused attention on their suitability for their roles. Just three days before Princess Anne married Tim Laurence, the separation of the Prince and Princess of Wales was announced simultaneously by Buckingham Palace and by Prime Minister John Major in the House of Commons. The timing seemed extraordinary and baffled commentators – although the official explanation was that it was made to clear the air before the young princes, William and Harry, came home from school for Christmas – but even more baffling was the Prime Minister's statement that:

The succession to the throne is unaffected. The children of the Prince and Princess retain their position in the line of succession and there is no reason why the Princess of Wales should not be crowned Queen in due course. The Prince of Wales's succession as head of the Church of England is also unaffected.

The immediate and popular reaction was to wonder how a couple who were unable any longer to live together could possibly share the throne with any degree of success. Historians pointed out, however, that a distant marital relationship had not proved any barrier to an effective reign in the past – as long as both partners were prepared to play the part allotted to them. The real problems will begin if either Charles or Diana decide they want the freedom to marry someone else, a not unlikely event. It is hard to see how a divorced Charles could ascend the throne and become titular head of a church that still has difficulty in countenancing divorce.

One of the most interesting and essential qualities of the British monarchy, however, has been its adaptability. It may seem a little fossilized at the moment, and out of touch with the 1990s, but in previous generations it has shown over and over again its ability to reconstruct itself in tune with the times. Individual representatives may prove less than ideally suited to the job. Ethelred the Redeless in the tenth century thought he could control the Danes who were hammering at the gate, but he was wrong, and England for a time became part of a Scandinavian empire under the Danish king Cnut. Edward II thought he could run the kingdom for his own pleasure. He too was wrong, and was murdered for his pains, but his son Edward III was a stalwart and successful king.

ABOVE: *The Braemar Games is one of the few public engagements allowed to disturb the prolonged family holiday at Balmoral.*

Charles I considered that the 'divinity that doth hedge a king', in Shakespeare's immortal phrase, entitled him to instant obedience and whatever taxes he chose to levy. Oliver Cromwell and an executioner's axe proved him wrong, but the Commonwealth lasted less than twenty years and then Charles's son, Charles II, a merry but circumspect monarch, was back on the throne. The monarchy has survived the Glorious Revolution, when Charles II's brother James II was deposed in favour of his daughter Mary and her Dutch husband William of Orange; it has survived a German king (George I) who spoke no English; a mad king (the unfortunate George III); and a possibly bigamous king, George IV, who contracted a morganatic marriage with a commoner before his debts forced him into a more practical union with a foreign princess, Caroline of Brunswick. The relationship was such a disaster that when George was crowned in 1820 he refused to involve Caroline in the ceremony, and London was treated to the elevating spectacle of the future Queen trying to gain access to Westminster Abbey for her own coronation. On George's death his brother William came to the throne as William IV, the Sailor King, and proved a sensible and flexible monarch – despite his longterm liaison with an actress, by whom he had ten illegitimate children. His failure to provide a royal heir led to the accession of Victoria.

The individual representatives clearly do not define the institution, or in the face of all these complications it would have collapsed long since. In fact in the present Queen the British Crown has one of its most respected and experienced heads of state. As monarch for over forty years, Queen Elizabeth II has seen the public image of her family revolutionized; as one astute chronicler of the House of Windsor put it:

As a human story and a super-human dream remorselesly conveyed throughout the world by all the means of modern mass communications, the monarchy is more than ever indispensable, and probably immortal.

Perhaps the problem that the Windsors face at the moment is not so much to do with their own achievements or otherwise, but with exactly that super-human dream, which they themselves invited their admiring public to dream. The mystique of the model royal family, as reinforcing the symbolic influence of the monarchy, has proved painfully illusory. For the monarchy to survive and to continue to play its role, we need once again to separate the private from the public man and woman. The test of any dignitary's – or indeed any employee's – suitability for his or her job is whether or not he carries out his role adequately, not whether his family is intact, how his relatives behave, or whether his private behaviour is impeccable. In her Guildhall speech the Queen seemed to indicate that she felt the time was ripe to subject the role of the monarchy to public scrutiny, and that this process 'could and should act as an effective engine for change.' If this invitation to debate the style of monarchy that Britain wishes to enjoy in the 21st century is taken up, we may yet see that flexible institution survive to regard the troubles of the 1990s as a minor hiccup in a thousand years of history.

QUEEN REGNANT

LEFT: *State visits abroad supposedly serve a valuable purpose in boosting Britain's export performance, but there are no hard and fast trade statistics to support the once fashionable view that trade follows the Crown. In terms of diplomatic prestige, however, the Queen's travels are considerably more effective. Here she is seen on walkabout in Beijing in 1986, attended by the then Foreign Secretary Sir Geoffrey Howe and an enthusiastic group of children.*

RIGHT: *On the Great Wall of China, the 1500-mile long fortification built in the third century BC to repel nomadic invasion from the north. Prince Philip's off-the-cuff remark about 'slitty-eyed foreigners' was regarded as evidence of the Royal Family's insensitivity to the offence that such clumsy jokiness can cause.*

BELOW: *Addressing Congress, Washington, 1991.*

Formal state occasions remain a staple of the British monarchy. In her 21st birthday message, six years before she acceded to the throne, the young Princess Elizabeth had indicated the high seriousness with which she viewed her role: 'I declare before you all that my whole life, whether it be long or short, shall be devoted to your service and the service of our great Imperial family to which we all belong . . . God help me make good my vow.' She has firmly resisted all suggestions that the Royal Family should abandon its old-fashioned and expensive pageantry and follow the example set by the egalitarian and casual Dutch royals.

LEFT: *The Queen takes the salute at the Trooping the Colour ceremony, the annual celebration in June of her official birthday. The ceremony has its origins in the parade of regimental flags, or Colours, so that foreign mercenaries serving in the royal army would learn to recognize them. It is now a military spectacular held on Horse Guards Parade in London, although the Queen no longer takes the salute on horseback.*

LEFT: *The State Opening of Parliament in October after the long summer recess is another opportunity for regal pomp. Here the Queen is seen arriving at the Houses of Parliament before reading the speech drafted for her by the Prime Minister and Cabinet of the day, outlining the government's plans for legislation in the forthcoming year. She gives the speech in the hereditary House of Lords rather than the elected House of Commons; no monarch has been permitted to enter the Commons since Charles I's attempt to imprison three MPs whom he believed had breached the royal prerogative.*

BELOW: *The Gulf Parade in 1991, to mark the return of British troops from the Gulf War, was a more sombre occasion.*

The Queen at work. The nineteenth-century constitutional historian Sir Walter Bagehot pointed out that: 'If we look at history we shall find that it is only during the period of the present reign (Queen Victoria) that in England the duties of a constitutional sovereign have ever been well performed . . .'

RIGHT: *A historic moment as the Supreme Head of the Church of England and Defender of the Faith meets the Supreme Pontiff, Pope John Paul II, head of the Catholic church.*

BELOW: *A glorious colour combination as the Queen inspects the Royal Welsh Fusiliers.*

FAR RIGHT: *Dressed in full regalia. Successive Prime Ministers have discovered that they need to be well briefed for their weekly meeting with their sovereign, who keeps a close eye on current events. Many have developed a warm and affectionate respect for their monarch.*

For their leisure activities the Royal Family share the traditional hunting, shooting and fishing interests of the landed gentry from which they ultimately stem. The Queen never goes abroad for pleasure, preferring to spend her holidays at her Scottish Highlands home of Balmoral Castle near Aberdeen, built by Prince Albert.

LEFT: *The Queen in typical countrywoman's wear of riding gear and headscarf at the Royal Windsor Horse Show.*

RIGHT: *Prince Philip was a keen polo player until increasing age and painful arthritis persuaded him to abandon the saddle in favour of the driving seat. Here he is seen taking part in four-in-hand driving trials in Windsor Great Park.*

BELOW: *A country family scene with the beagles: the Queen pictured in the early 1980s with (from left) her niece and nephew, Lady Sarah Armstrong-Jones and Viscount Linley, the Queen Mother and Prince Edward.*

LEFT: *The Prince of Wales and Prince Philip, Duke of Edinburgh, in their ceremonial bearskins for Trooping the Colour. A forceful, intelligent and reserved man, Prince Philip has not been an easy father. His determination to make his sons tough and manly worked well with the confident Andrew but was much less successful with his two more sensitive and imaginative sons.*

RIGHT AND BELOW: *Prince Philip as royal consort. He has compensated for his secondary role as husband of one monarch and father of the next by accumulating an impressive workload in his own right. He is president or honorary member of over 850 organizations, attends over 500 public functions annually and is perhaps best known for his chairmanship of the World Wide Fund for Nature. The media abounds periodically with rumors about his infidelity – always firmly ignored by the Palace – but after nearly 50 years his marriage gives the appearance of a settled, comfortable and supportive routine.*

LEFT *The Queen Mother is one of the best-loved and least controversial of the Windsors, always received rapturously as the 'nation's grandmother' on her rare public appearances. Ironically, however, it was her happy marriage to George VI, whose own childhood had been overshadowed by fear of his distant and dictatorial father George V, that started the myth of the ideal Royal Family. The Duchess of York, as she was before her husband's surprise accession to the throne after the Abdication Crisis, encouraged suitably deferential writers to record the everyday life of the happy household with its devoted parents and two charming daughters. In this case the happiness and devotion were real enough.*

LEFT: *The Queen Mother's birthday on 4 August has become a day for happy and informal celebrations, and her 90th birthday in 1990 was marked by an outbreak of real public affection. Here she is seen greeting wellwishers in Wales at the start of the festivities and collecting armfuls of daffodils, the Welsh national emblem.*

BELOW: *The birthday is always recorded by an informal photograph session at the gates of the Queen Mother's home, Clarence House in London. Pictured with her on her 92nd birthday in 1992 are (from left) the Queen Mother, the Queen, and Princess Margaret, with Charles and Princess Margaret's son David Linley in serious discussion behind them, and Diana and Harry, with Andrew half hidden.*

RIGHT, FAR RIGHT AND BELOW:
The Queen Mother's dignified public facade covers a robust attitude to life. At lunch once, when the Queen, unusually for her, accepted a second glass of wine, the Queen Mother is supposed to have said: 'I shouldn't if I were you, dear. After all, you do have to reign all afternoon.' The preparations for her 90th birthday celebrations were marred by a telltale article by author and journalist A N Wilson, then a regular guest at the private dinner parties the Queen Mother enjoys hosting, who broke the unwritten rule that royal guests never discuss their hosts by revealing that the Queen Mother worries about money, dislikes Princess Michael of Kent and enjoys detective novels. Ironically the gossip rebounded on the gossipmonger, and Wilson was roundly denounced in the press for his disloyalty.

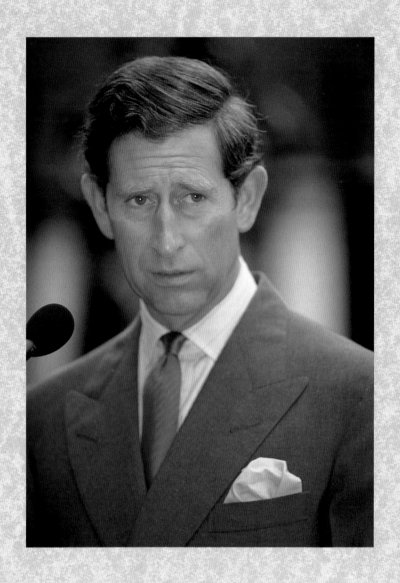

HEIRS APPARENT

ABOVE: *The Prince of Wales pictured in July 1992, a time when private negotiations about his failed marriage were at their height; his solemn face shows the strain.*

RIGHT: *Prince Charles attends his grandmother, with whom he enjoys a close and loving relationship, at the Garter ceremony at St George's Chapel, Windsor Castle.*

PREVIOUS PAGES: *Educated at Gordonstoun, the tough Scottish boarding school which his father had attended, Charles followed Prince Philip into the Royal Navy after two years at Trinity College, Cambridge, and developed a daredevil streak as deep-sea diver, helicopter pilot and parachutist. He is fundamentally a solitary man, however, whose childhood was overshadowed by his mother's royal duties and who has never enjoyed a relaxed relationship with his demanding and impatient father.*

LEFT: *Charles at the controls of a Chieftain tank at Tidworth army camp, Hampshire.*

RIGHT: *As colonel-in-chief of the Parachute Regiment at the D-Day anniversary celebrations in France.*

FAR LEFT: *Charles inaugurated as a native American chief, with full headdress. Once asked by an interviewer when he had realized that he was the heir to the throne, he replied: 'I think it's something that dawns on you with the most ghastly inexorable sense . . . slowly you get the idea that you have a certain duty and responsibility.'*

LEFT: *In relaxed and thoughtful mood, with an affectionate pony nuzzling at his hand, Charles seems most at home.*

BELOW: *Another solitary occupation favoured by the Prince of Wales is fly fishing, a slow and absorbing sport. Here he makes his cast in a Highland pool.*

ABOVE: *Charles pictured at the inevitable polo match, one of those sports in which only rich people participate, with Lord Mountbatten of Burma, a seminal influence on the young prince, and Princess Michael of Kent. Earl Mountbatten, formerly Lord Louis, was the son of Queen Victoria's grand-daughter Victoria of Hesse and Prince Louis of Battenberg. Despite a distinguished career in the Royal Navy, Prince Louis was made the object of anti-German feeling during World War I, and changed his name to Mountbatten. His daughter Alice married Prince Andrew of Greece, a less than successful relationship which produced four daughters and then, finally, Prince Philip, the present Duke of Edinburgh. His son Louis, both Philip and Charles's beloved Uncle Dickie, followed the paternal footsteps into the Royal Navy, served with distinction as the last Viceroy of India (before independence, 1947), and then as Governor-General.*

RIGHT: *Mountbatten's funeral. His murder by IRA bomb in August 1979 brought politics very close to the Royal Family.*

RIGHT: *Charles at a polo match with Camilla Parker-Bowles, the married woman whose relationship with the Prince of Wales was believed to be behind much of Princess Diana's unhappiness; a belief substantiated by the 'Camillagate' tapes, which revealed that the pair were longterm lovers. Camilla Shand, lively daughter of a wealthy wine merchant who also served as Deputy Lord Lieutenant of East Sussex, first met Prince Charles in 1972, and announced her engagement to Andrew Parker-Bowles soon after Charles went to sea with the Royal Navy in spring 1973. They continued to meet, however, and Camilla accompanied Charles to Zimbabwe in 1980 as his official escort for the country's independence celebrations, as well as on more private trips, such as a painting holiday in Florence in 1991.*

BELOW LEFT: *Another loyal and supportive female friend is Dale, Lady Tryon, invariably known as Kanga, seen here resplendent in off-the-shoulder black velvet accompanying Prince Charles to the Diamond Ball.*

BELOW RIGHT: *The Prince's Trust, a charitable foundation aimed to foster self-help schemes in deprived inner-city areas, is Charles's response to the Duke of Edinburgh Award Scheme established by his father.*

THE PRINCE'S TRUST

THE PRINCE'S TRUST

LEFT: *The marriage of the Prince of Wales to the 20-year-old Lady Diana Spencer seemed an ideal choice; she came from the same sheltered, aristocratic background, seemed a gentle, malleable character, and was devoted to children. The previous six months had been stressful ones for her, as she dodged the media and began to learn what was expected of royalty – without much help from the Palace establishment. The gloriously romantic wedding dress had to be taken in several times as the bride-to-be grew thinner with the strain. Sadly the fairytale swiftly proved illusory; Diana could not fulfil her husband's need for intellectual companionship, and Charles was baffled and irritated by Diana's emotional demands and mood-swings.*

LEFT: *The christening of Prince William Arthur Philip Louis, who was born on 21 June, 1982, just eleven months after the wedding; Prince Henry Charles Albert David followed in September 1984. Diana was a devoted mother and tried to ensure that during her sons' early years they lived a normal school life and saw as much as possible of their parents.*

BELOW: *Trooping the Colour guarantees a large royal turnout, and is known to family members as an 'MOBG' occasion; morally obliged to go. This relaxed family scene was caught in 1989 as the balcony party gazed up at the fly past: from left, Princess Margaret and Princess Diana share a joke, with Princess Alexandra behind and William and Harry in front, while Prince Charles, the Queen and Prince Philip look skyward.*

LEFT: *In the early days of marriage the Waleses seemed devoted to each other, and were happy to demonstrate their affection. Here the winner of a polo match earns a kiss.*

BELOW: *Even at the start there were inevitable strains, however; Diana resented Charles's other friendships and what she saw as his coldness towards their children, while Charles, after many years of bachelor independence, found it hard to respond to the demands of a full-time relationship.*

RIGHT: *The stresses became increasingly apparent in the late 1980s and early 1990s and caused endless media speculation. This tense scene took place in Egypt, spring 1992.*

BELOW RIGHT: *Distant communication in Canada, 1991; presumably it is intended that this formal working relationship will continue now the couple are separated.*

RIGHT: *Thailand 1988: royal tours attract a horde of attentive press photographers and require detailed and arduous planning. It was on their first joint tour, Australia in 1982, that it dawned on Prince Charles that his shy wife might develop into a bigger media star than himself.*

BELOW: *Diana also developed an assured and stylish dress sense; this zingy red and violet outfit features two of her favourite colours. Her sylphlike figure supports the rumours about an eating disorder.*

BELOW RIGHT: *Similar colours for an evening dress on the Thai tour.*

RIGHT: *Diana's first major solo foreign tour was to Pakistan in 1991, and with hindsight can be seen as a significant turning point in her evolution into an independent princess.*

OVERLEAF: *A colourful scene in India in February 1992, as Diana is escorted by dancers in traditional dress. The Princess was accused of media manipulation when she organized a poignant photo shoot of herself alone in front of the Taj Mahal while Prince Charles pursued his duties elsewhere.*

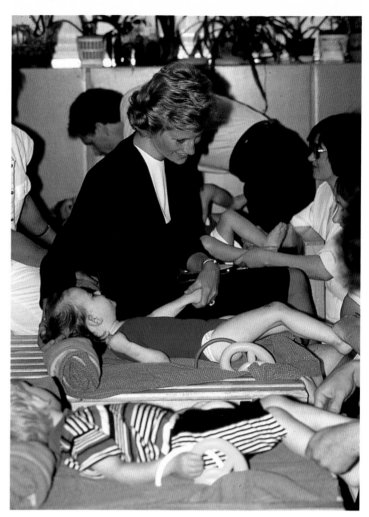

FAR LEFT ABOVE: *One of Diana's greatest gifts is her warm-hearted ability to respond to the individuals she meets. This has become increasingly valuable as she has moved into the fund-raising and charitable activities beloved of rich, under-occupied women. Surrounded by the nuns of Mother Teresa's hospital in Calcutta, Diana is relaxed and at ease.*

LEFT ABOVE: *While in Budapest, Hungary, in spring 1992, Diana visited the Peto Institute, which specializes in therapy for children born with severe cerebral palsy. Again she is instantly a member of the group, sitting on the floor and holding hands.*

LEFT BELOW: *Diana on her own in Egypt in front of the magnificent pyramids.*

RIGHT: *Elegant in a palest pink, pearl-embroidered evening dress on her solo Pakistan trip; the long scarf is a tactful gesture to local customs.*

LEFT: *Diana, perhaps surprisingly, is Colonel-in-Chief of a number of regiments, including the Royal Hampshires, the 13th/18th Royal Hussars and the Princess of Wales Own Regiment of Canada. Here she investigates the controls of a tank with her usual charm.*

RIGHT: *Meeting the crowd in Taunton, Somerset, Diana carries a gift of grape hyacinths that tone with her blue suit.*

BELOW: *Playing the piano for Czech orphans at Prague Castle during an official tour in spring 1991.*

RIGHT: *One of the areas of conflict between Charles and Diana was holidays. The Queen's timetable is rigid: Christmas at Sandringham, spring at Buckingham Palace, Easter at Windsor, the summer season in London, then two months at Balmoral from August to October. The family is expected to follow a similar pattern, but Diana found the extended stay at Balmoral, with its bracing and inflexible atmosphere, more than she could bear. Holidays with the Spanish royal family at the Marivent Palace on Mallorca are far more to her taste.*

BELOW: *Skiing was a taste that Charles and Diana shared, and Diana first asserted her independent character when she got tired of co-operating with intrusive photographers on the ski slopes above Klosters. She has not returned to Klosters since the tragic accident that killed royal aide Major Hugh Lindsay; here she and the two young princes enjoy the Austrian snow.*

RIGHT: *When interviewed by veteran television personality Alastair Burnet in 1985, the Princess of Wales modestly described her role as 'supporting my husband whenever I can . . . and also, most important, being a mother and wife'. While it was painfully clear long before the separation that Diana no longer felt able to support her husband, there is no dispute about the close and loving relationship between her and her sons, with whom she continues to spend as much time as possible. This spray-soaked shot was taken at the Niagara Falls, Canada, in October 1991.*

RIGHT: *The young princes at the Windsor Horse Show. They are never alone for a moment, and every effort has been made to shield them from the press revelations of the last year. Total isolation is impossible, however, particularly since the Waleses agreed that their boys should attend pre-prep and prep schools rather than be educated at home in the early years. Both are now boarders at Ludgrove in Berkshire.*

BELOW: *Leaving Canada on board the royal yacht* Britannia, *the young royals wave dutifully.*

LEFT: *Mother and sons in Canada, the boys dressed in toning outfits in maroon and black and matching shirts. They have just surveyed the Niagara Falls, and their hair is still wet from the spray.*

BELOW: *Harry and the Queen Mother, with Diana almost hidden by the Queen Mum's inevitable floral hat, in the carriage parade at Trooping the Colour, summer 1992.*

CHILDREN AND GRANDCHILDREN

ABOVE: *Princess Anne's marriage to Captain Mark Phillips in 1973 – the first royal wedding in the younger generation – seemed an ideal match between two dedicated and dashing equestrians, although not all Anne's relations were enthusiastic about the man whom friends cruelly nicknamed 'Fog' – thick and wet. In this balcony shot, Lady Sarah Armstrong-Jones and Prince Edward are bridesmaid and pageboy respectively.*

LEFT: *After a couple of years at Sandhurst, where Mark was an army instructor, the Phillipses set up home at Gatcombe Park in Gloucestershire, a £5 million gift from the Queen. Although Anne had a Civil List allowance, Mark always made a point of having to earn his own living.*

RIGHT: *Anne travels worldwide in her role as President of the Save the Children Fund; here she is in the Sudan.*

RIGHT: *It was Anne's work with Save the Children that earned her the respect of the world's press, which until the mid-1980s had viewed her as spoilt and unco-operative. Her father's daughter and very much his favourite child, she shares both his intelligence – she passed five O-levels and two A-levels at Benenden, the exclusive girls' school she attended – and his intolerance. An Australian photographer who urged her to 'Look over here, my love,' was well snubbed for his impertinence. Save the Children has harnessed her robust self-confidence, her energy and her commitment to a wholly worthy cause.*

BELOW: *Anne at an Asian family centre in London. She may not provoke the same immediate rapport and affection as her glamorous sister-in-law, but perhaps she earns more lasting respect for her less well-publicized work.*

RIGHT: *The Save the Children Fund has been active for several years in the Sudan, where a combination of famine and civil war has left large sections of the population destitute. Anne's tours of inspection to this and similarly disaster-struck areas have generated a substantial flow of financial and practical help.*

LEFT: *The water jump at the Badminton horse trials. Throughout her childhood and youth Princess Anne was a keen and competitive horsewoman, because 'It has nothing to do with my position. If I am good at it, I'm good at it – and not because I am Princess Anne.' In 1971 she proved she was good at it by winning the European Three-Day Event Championship, and in 1976 was selected for the British team at the Olympic Games in Montreal.*

BELOW: *Anne in the colourful silks of the jump jockey. Horse racing remains a largely male preserve and it took considerable persistence before this determined group of women were allowed to participate.*

RIGHT: *Anne attends Ascot in 1987 escorted by Commander Timothy Laurence. From the mid-1980s the Phillips marriage, once billed as the egalitarian fairytale of the princess and the commoner, was effectively over. Anne's royal duties and Mark's increasingly demanding business enterprises gradually proved incompatible. Naval officer Tim Laurence had first gone to work as the Queen's equerry in 1986; in April 1989 he was named as the writer of four personal letters stolen from the Princess. The contents of these were never revealed, although described at the time as 'affectionate'; the Queen refused to accept her equerry's resignation and Tim Laurence himself preserved a discreet silence. Four months later it was announced that Anne and Mark were to separate.*

BELOW: *Anne and Mark have remained good friends, united in their love of their two children, Zara and Peter, despite the scandal of an alleged paternity suit brought against Mark by a New Zealand art teacher in March 1991.*

RIGHT: *Tim Laurence at the Royal Windsor Horse Show; although his own background is solidly middle-class, his career both in the Navy and in the Royal Household has equipped him with the necessary qualities of charm, discretion and savoir-faire to accommodate himself to the strains of living with royalty. His relationship with Princess Anne had already survived five years before their wedding was announced in December 1992, and he is treated by the Windsors as one of the family.*

BELOW: *HRH The Princess Royal, Mrs Timothy Laurence, and her husband on their first official engagement as a married couple, the opening of the Bolshoi Ballet's season at the Royal Albert Hall. Anne is radiant in glorious shot silk, and Tim glows with quiet pride.*

RIGHT: *Peter and Zara Phillips lead a comfortable country existence at Gatcombe Park when not at school. Peter, aged 14, is a pupil at the tough Scottish boarding school Gordonstoun, which all three of his uncles attended, while Zara attends Port Regis prep school in Dorset. Conservative royalists were shocked, at Peter's birth, that the Queen's grandson should be plain Master Phillips, but his father had firmly refused to accept a title and, by the curious rules of British genealogy, he acquires no status from his mother.*

RIGHT: *Prince Andrew, created Duke of York at the time of his marriage to Sarah Ferguson, seemed to many to be the most robust and least complex of the Queen's sons. The demanding regime at Gordonstoun suited him better than either of his brothers – though, interestingly, he was the only one not to be made head boy – and he moved straight on to naval training at Dartmouth Naval College in Devon. The discipline suited him; 'When I'm at sea I feel six inches taller,' he is quoted as saying, 'One can ignore all that is going on in the rest of the world and get on with one's job.'*

BELOW: *Andrew is welcomed home from the Falklands War by the Queen, the Duke of Edinburgh and Princess Anne. As a trained helicopter pilot, his role was to use his Sea King helicopter as a decoy to protect* HMS Invincible *from Argentinian Exocets. He served with gallantry and helped to rescue from death the crew of the supply ship* Atlantic Conveyor *but, like many a returning war hero, found it difficult to settle to peacetime existence.*

RIGHT: *Andrew in his Sea King.*

LEFT: *Andrew as family man; he and Sarah have two daughters, Beatrice and Eugenie. Here Eugenie rides on her father's shoulders and puts a firm hand in his eye. Appearances are deceptive, however; in 1990 Andrew spent just 42 nights with his family. After some years as a flying instructor, he decided to go back to sea, and the resulting long absences put inevitable strains on the marriage. It was during one of these absences that Sarah holidayed first in North Africa and then in the south of France with Texan millionaire Steve Wyatt, a holiday that was to sow the seeds of scandal and divorce when Wyatt's photographs came to light some 18 months later.*

BELOW: *Andrew pays a formal visit to* HMS Campbeltown *with his wife and mother.*

RIGHT: *Andrew and Fergie in boisterous form with a jereboam of champagne at a clay pigeon shoot. After some of the more outrageous liaisons that Andrew had formed in the past, including a close eighteen-month relationship with former soft porn star turned photographer Koo Stark, Sarah Ferguson, daughter of Prince Charles's polo manager, seemed eminently suitable and the romance was actively encouraged by the Royal Family. At first she was seen as a breath of fresh air in the stuffy corridors of Windsor and Balmoral, but her cheerful spontaneity soon landed her in trouble, which the Palace was not too concerned to help her out of. In the early days of marriage she came under attack for her dress sense – or lack of it – her vulgarity and her weight, as well for leaving the infant Beatrice behind when she and Andrew went on tour to Australia. Just the same the announcement of her separation from Andrew, in March 1992, came as a shock to most commentators, and seemed to be more Sarah's than Andrew's decision. Like her sister-in-law Diana, she was giving up on the Royal Family, and much was written about the Windsor men's inability to forge loving, supportive, permanent relationships. The breaking of the John Bryan story in the summer, and the photographs of a topless Fergie cavorting with another Texan millionaire, redressed the balance.*

LEFT: *A distinctly unflattering photograph of Charles and Andrew in morning suit for the wedding of their second cousin, Lady Helen Windsor, daughter of the Duke and Duchess of Kent. The marriage took place in July 1992; Andrew was already separated from his wife, Charles's marriage was drawing to a close.*

BELOW: *Sarah moved out of the much-criticized ranch-style family home that she and Andrew had had built at Sunninghill, Berkshire, within hours of the separation being announced, and took up residence in a small house nearby. Unlike her strong-minded sister-in-law, she shows no signs of trying to maintain an independent royal role for herself.*

LEFT: *The Duke and Duchess of York in evening dress shortly before the announcement of their separation. Fergie cuts a more elegant figure than in the early days of her marriage, but her dress sense remains unreliable, witness the extraordinary ruffle of red satin.*

RIGHT: *Prince Edward stunned the stuffier members of the royal set when he accepted a menial job as trainee production assistant with Andrew Lloyd Webber's Really Useful Theatre Company, but seemed to have found the right metier. Sadly he was out of a job within a couple of years when the company was rationalized, and has not found a similar niche.*

BELOW: *Edward with his father. After Gordonstoun and a couple of years teaching in New Zealand, he took a degree in archaeology, anthropology and history at the University of Cambridge, and then announced his intention of joining the elite fighting force of the Royal Marines as a trainee. Prince Philip, honorary Captain-General of the Marines, was delighted, as were the Marines themselves to have been preferred to the Senior Service, the Navy, by a member of the Royal Family. The experience was an unhappy one, however, and Edward left the Marines without even completing his 34-week training period as an officer cadet.*

RIGHT: *At the wedding of his cousin Helen Windsor, Edward already looks anxious and middle-aged.*

THE EXTENDED FAMILY

ABOVE: *Princess Margaret
glorious in fuchsia pink.*

RIGHT: *The marriage of Lady
Helen Windsor to Tim Taylor.*

LEFT: *Princess Margaret and former husband Lord Snowdon at the opera. In the early 1950s she fell in love with a divorced man 16 years her senior, Group Captain Peter Townsend, a much decorated fighter pilot, but the obstacles placed in the path of their marriage, proved too much. A few years later her engagement to photographer Anthony Armstrong-Jones seemed a charming story of princess and commoner united by their interest in the arts, but the marriage proved quite as explosive, though rather less well publicized, than that of Charles and Diana. In 1978 they were the first royals to divorce for over a century. Only Snowdon has remarried.*

BELOW LEFT: *Lady Sarah Armstrong-Jones, Margaret's daughter, is a popular and likable royal.*

BELOW: *David, Viscount Linley has carved out a career for himself as a restaurant-owner and maker of fine furniture.*

RIGHT: *A delightful family group at the formal celebration of the Queen's 60th birthday in 1986.*

ABOVE LEFT: *It took the Duke of Kent four years to persuade Katharine Worsley, daughter of the Lord Lieutenant of the North Riding of Yorkshire, to marry him. The wedding took place in 1961 in York Minster, suitably enough, and Princess Anne was chief bridesmaid.*

ABOVE: *Edward, Duke of Kent, the Queen's first cousin; his father George, Duke of Kent, who married the charming and much loved Princess Marina of Greece, was the younger brother of Edward VIII and George VI. The young Edward made a promising career in the army until his royal connection made him a security hazard on active service in Ireland. Instead he has carved a valuable career as Vice-Chairman of the British Overseas Trade Board.*

LEFT: *Lady Helen Windsor was the second Kent child, born in 1964, a good year for royalty: Princess Alexandra's son James Ogilvy and Princess Margaret's daughter Lady Sarah Armstrong-Jones were born in the same year. In summer 1992 she in turn married commoner Tim Taylor.*

LEFT: *Birgitte, Duchess of Gloucester. Richard, Duke of Gloucester was in fact the quiet younger son; his dashing older brother William was an enthusiastic pilot and died tragically in an airplane accident. Richard had meanwhile qualified as an architect at Cambridge, where he met and married the Danish Birgitte van Deurs, who was taking a language course there.*

BELOW LEFT: *A more controversial royal bride is Princess Michael of Kent, married to the Duke of Kent's younger brother Prince Michael. She was not only a Catholic but had also been married previously, and the marriage in 1978 was a civil ceremony.*

BELOW: *Since his marriage Prince Michael has grown a beard much like that of his grandfather Edward VII. He and Marie-Christine, known to the closed royal circle as Val, the blonde Valkyrie, have two children, Lord Frederick and Lady Gabriella Windsor.*

FAR LEFT: *Prince and Princess Michael at Ascot, 1991; she is well known for her determination to participate in royal life.*

LEFT: *The younger generation on their own. Lady Sarah Armstrong-Jones; Lady Helen Windsor; her younger brother Lord Nicholas Windsor; and Marina Ogilvy.*

BELOW LEFT: *Marina Ogilvy, daughter of Princess Alexandra and Sir Angus Ogilvy – who anticipated Mark Phillips in refusing a title on marrying into the Royal Family – caused a stir in 1989 when she announced her pregnancy but refused to marry the father of her baby, curiously named Zenouska. In the end she did marry Paul Mowatt, but has continued to cultivate headlines.*

BELOW: *Princess Alexandra, younger sister of the Duke of Kent and so also the Queen's cousin, a quiet and popular royal who carries out a full programme of public engagements.*